The Nature Kid's Guide to COBRAS

DAVID ANDERSON

LP Media Inc. Publishing

For information address LP Media Inc. Publishing,
30012 Variolite St NW, Princeton MN 55371
www.lpmedia.org

Publication Data

Cobras
The Nature Kid's Guide to Cobras — First edition.

Summary: "Learn all about Cobras, the Nature Kid Way"
— Provided by publisher.

ISBN: 979-8-89818-230-4

[1. Cobras – Non-Fiction] I. Title.

Title: The Nature Kid's Guide to Cobras

CONTENTS

SNEAKY SPOTS

A group of cobras is called a quiver — just like a case full of arrows!

Hiss! An Indian cobra eases out from under a flat rock.

Cobras live in many warm places. You can find them in forests, fields, and near old buildings. They love spots with shade and hiding holes.

Indian cobras often live close to farms. Why? Mice come to eat the crops. And cobras come to eat the mice! That is why people sometimes see these snakes near their homes.

Cobras need warm spots to keep their bodies going. They search for places where the sun heats the ground. A cozy hiding spot with nearby sunshine makes the perfect cobra home.

COBRA COUNTRY

FUN FACT!

Cobras live on two continents — but not a single one lives wild in North or South America!

Whoosh! A king cobra glides through a jungle in India.

Cobras are found in Africa and Asia. That covers a lot of the world! They live in hot, green jungles and dry, sandy deserts.

King cobras call the forests of Southeast Asia home. They like thick jungles with lots of rain. Indian cobras and other species prefer dry grasslands and scrublands where the sun beats down all day.

You will not find wild cobras in cold places. They must live where the sun shines strong. No matter where they settle, if the land stays warm, cobras have found a way to survive there.

SIZE UP

A king cobra can raise its head up to six feet off the ground — high enough to look a person in the eye!

Hissss! A king cobra uncoils across the forest floor, stretching out long.

King cobras are the longest venomous snakes on Earth. They can grow up to 18 feet long! That is as long as three bikes lined up in a row.

Most cobras are much smaller. Many measure four to six feet long, about as tall as a grown-up standing straight. Even these smaller cobras look huge when they spread their hoods.

Cobras can weigh up to 20 pounds. Even the big ones are slim and light. Their thin bodies help them move fast and squeeze into tight spaces.

COOL COILS

An Indian cobra's hood has markings that look like a pair of eyeglasses — some people call it the spectacled cobra!

Ssss! A cobra spreads its wide hood to look bigger than it is.

Cobras are known for their big, flat **hoods**. The hood is made of long ribs that spread out like an umbrella. It makes the snake look much bigger and scarier than it really is.

A cobra's body is covered in smooth, dry scales. The scales overlap like tiles on a roof, protecting the snake from scrapes as it slides along rough ground.

Cobras have sharp **fangs** near the front of their mouths. Venom flows through the fangs when they bite. Those fangs are the cobra's most powerful tool.

SENSE IT

Cobras cannot hear music — snake charmers fool them with movement, not sound!

Flick! A cobra's forked tongue tastes the air for prey.

Cobras use their tongues to smell the world. A forked tongue flicks in and out fast, sometimes 200 times per minute! It picks up tiny bits of scent from the air.

Cobras can feel shaking in the ground. They do not have ears on the outside of their heads. Instead, they sense sounds through their jawbones pressed against the earth.

Monocled cobras hunt at night. Their eyes work well in the dark. This sharp night vision helps them find frogs and mice long after sunset.

DEADLY DEFENSE

14

Splat! A Mozambique spitting cobra shoots venom from its mouth!

Cobras have many ways to scare off danger. First, they lift their heads high. Then they spread their hoods wide to look big and scary.

Spitting cobras can spray venom from their fangs. They aim right for the eyes! The venom can hit a target up to eight feet away with amazing accuracy.

If a cobra hisses, it means stay back. That loud sound is a final warning. Most cobras would rather scare you away than fight.

MUNCH MENU

16

Gulp! A king cobra swallows a whole snake for lunch.

Most cobras eat small animals. Rats, mice, frogs, and lizards are all on the menu. Some also gobble up bird eggs and fish.

King cobras are special. Their name says it all! They eat other snakes, even other cobras. That is what makes them the king of all cobras.

Cobras swallow their food whole. They do not chew at all. Their stretchy jaws can open wide enough to fit meals much bigger than their own heads.

STRIKE FAST

A cobra can strike and pull back in less than one-tenth of a second — faster than you can blink!

Shhh! An Egyptian cobra is curled and ready to strike.

Cobras are sneaky hunters. They hide and wait for prey to come close. When the time is right, they strike in a flash.

A bite sends venom into the prey. The venom works fast. In just minutes, the animal cannot move. Then the cobra moves in and collects its meal.

Egyptian cobras often hunt at dusk. The low light helps them sneak up on prey without being seen. They creep close to rats and birds, then strike before their target can escape.

WATCH OUT

A mongoose has thick fur and special blood that helps protect it from cobra venom!

Dodge! A mongoose darts and spins around a cobra, waiting for the perfect moment to strike.

Even scary cobras have enemies. Hawks and eagles swoop in from the sky. Wild boars and big monitor lizards hunt them on the ground.

But the mongoose is the cobra's biggest foe. It is quick and brave. A mongoose can dodge a cobra's strikes again and again until the snake gets tired.

Indian cobras and mongooses have been fierce enemies for a very long time. When they meet, both get ready to fight. The mongoose wins most of the time thanks to its lightning speed.

STAY SAFE

A cobra can hold so still that birds sometimes land right next to it without noticing!

22

Zoom! A cape cobra races away from a big, hungry eagle!

Cobras try to avoid a fight when they can. Slipping away is always the first choice. They slide into holes, bushes, or tall grass before trouble starts.

Cape cobras are very fast movers. They can race across open land at high speed to escape danger. For them, running beats fighting every time.

Some cobras hide in water to get away. Others climb trees to reach safe spots high above the ground. A clever cobra always knows the best escape route.

SLITHER ON
DID YOU KNOW?
King cobras can slither at speeds of up to 12 miles per hour — faster than most people can run!
24

Swish! A cobra slides along the dusty ground like a rope.

Cobras do not have legs, but they move well. They push against the ground with their belly scales. Each scale grips the earth and pushes the snake forward.

Most cobras move in an S-shaped path. Their bodies curve side to side as they go. This wavy motion is how most snakes travel on flat ground.

King cobras can also swim. They glide through water using the same wavy motion they use on land. Streams and rivers are no problem for these amazing snakes.

DAY LIFE

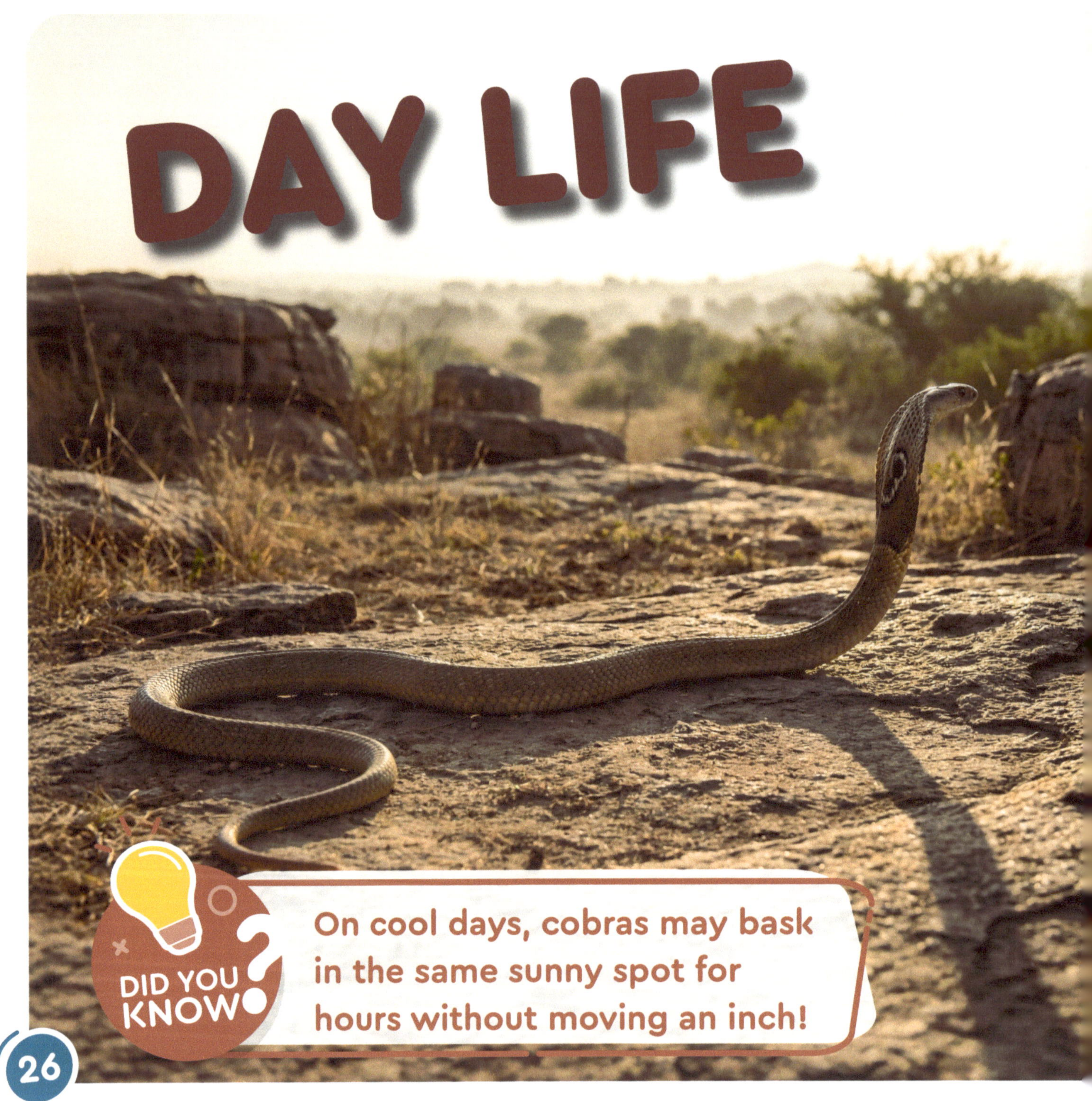

On cool days, cobras may bask in the same sunny spot for hours without moving an inch!

Rustle! A cobra warms its long body in the morning sun.

Cobras start the day by soaking up the sun. They are **cold-blooded**. That means they need heat from outside to warm up their muscles and get moving.

After warming up, cobras look for food. They may travel far to find a meal. When the day gets too hot, they rest in cool shade.

At night, most cobras find a safe spot to sleep. They curl up under rocks or in hollow logs. A quiet night of rest keeps a cobra healthy and ready to hunt again.

SOLO SNAKES

FUN FACT!
A single cobra needs a big area to live in — sometimes over 400 acres!

Slither! A lone cobra slides off through the tall grass.

Cobras like to be alone. They do not live in groups or packs. Each cobra hunts and sleeps on its own.

Two cobras may cross paths now and then. But they rarely stop for long. They simply go their own way without a second look.

The only time cobras get close is during **mating** season. After they mate, each one goes off alone. Cobras are loners all year long, and that suits them just fine.

DANCE FIGHTS

Thwap! Two male king cobras rise up and push each other.

Male king cobras fight over females. They rise up tall and try to push each other down. It looks like a wild, twisting dance!

The winner gets to mate with the female. The loser slinks away. These fights look scary but do not hurt the snakes much. No biting is allowed.

Males follow scent trails left by females. They may travel miles to find a mate. Mating happens once a year for most cobras, usually in spring.

Male cobras can wrestle for over an hour before one finally gives up and slithers away!

TINY TERRORS

Cobra eggs need about 60 to 80 days of warmth before the babies are ready to hatch!

Crack! A baby cobra pokes its head out of a white egg.

Baby cobras hatch from eggs. A mother may lay 20 to 40 eggs at one time! The eggs are soft and leathery, not hard like chicken eggs.

Babies are tiny but ready to go. They can move and hunt right away. A newborn cobra is about 10 inches long, just a little shorter than a school ruler.

Young cobras already have venom in their fangs. Even a small bite can be strong. These tiny snakes are bold and dangerous from day one.

GO ALONE

King cobras are the only snakes in the whole world that build nests for their eggs!

Poof! The mother cobra slips away and leaves the nest.

Most cobra mothers do not stay with their young. They place the eggs in a safe spot and leave. The babies must figure things out all alone.

King cobras are different. The mother stays close to her eggs and guards them for weeks. She will charge at animals much bigger than herself to keep the eggs safe.

But even king cobra moms leave before the babies come out. Why? She might eat them by mistake! No cobra parent teaches its young to hunt or hide.

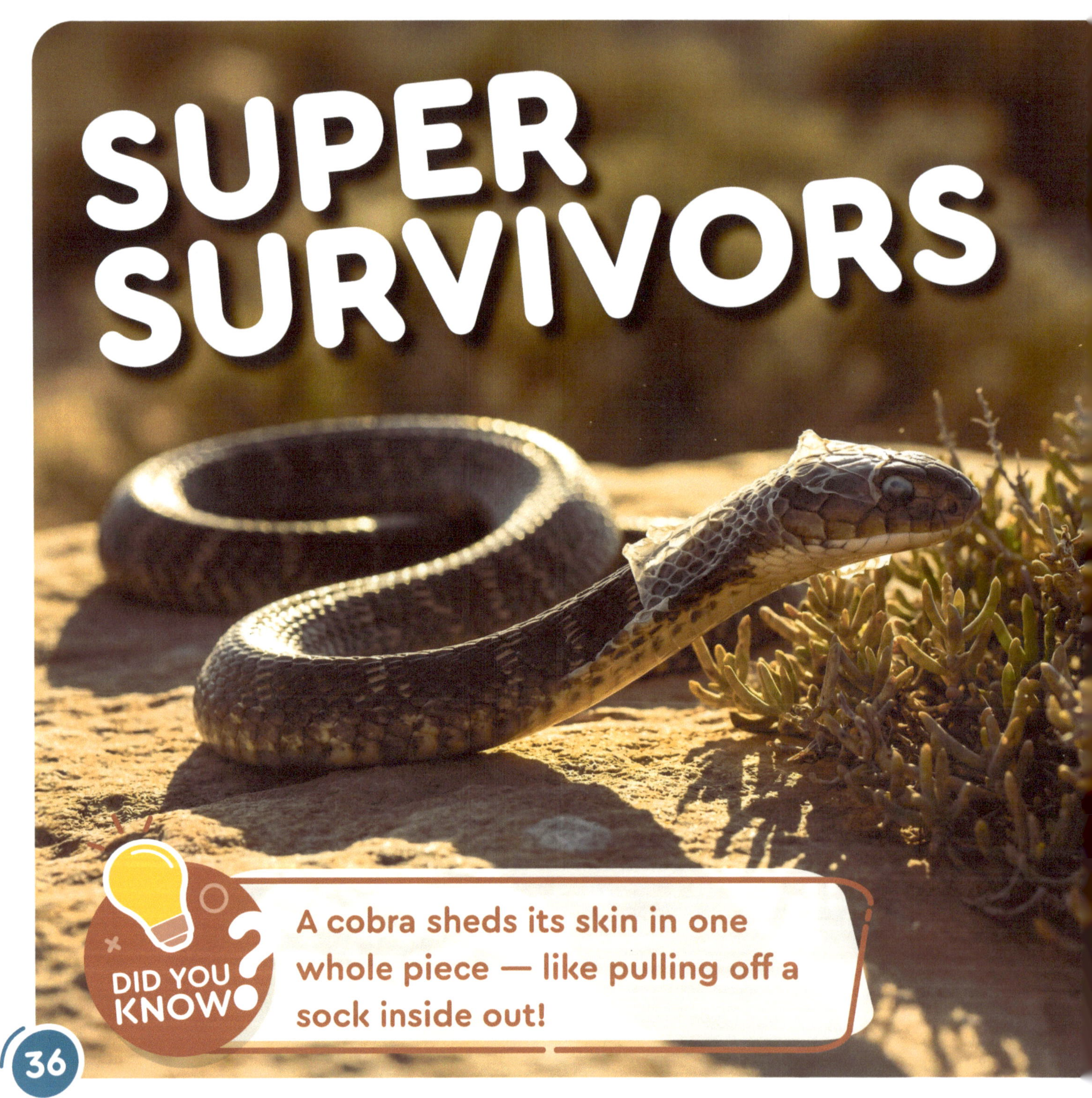

SUPER
SURVIVORS
DID YOU KNOW?
A cobra sheds its skin in one whole piece — like pulling off a sock inside out!
36

Crinkle! A cobra peels away its old, dry skin on a warm rock.

Cobras are ancient survivors. Their colors help them hide in grass, sand, and leaves. This trick is called **camouflage.**

Egyptian cobras are sandy brown. This helps them blend in with the dry desert ground. Predators walk right past without seeing them!

Cobras also shed their old skin a few times a year. A fresh set of scales keeps them healthy and free of bugs. Shedding is like getting a brand new coat every few months.

SAFE SPOTTING

Most cobras are more scared of people than people are of them — they just want to be left alone!

Shhh! A cape cobra rests on a sun-warmed boulder just off the trail.

Seeing a cobra in the wild is exciting! But always stay far away. Cobras are not pets, and they can be very dangerous.

If you are ever someplace cobras live and spot one, do not get close. Stay still and move back slowly. Never try to touch or pick up a wild snake, even if it looks calm.

Cape cobras live in South Africa where people hike. Park rangers know where cobras rest. Always listen to your guide and stay on the trail. That way, you can enjoy these amazing snakes from a safe distance.

GLOSSARY

camouflage

Colors or patterns that help an animal blend in and hide

cold-blooded

Having a body that cannot make its own heat

fangs

Long, sharp teeth that snakes use to bite

hood

The wide, flat skin behind a cobra's head

mating

When a male and female come together to make babies